WITHOUT MASKS

SARA LEITH-TANOUS

I can picture my father's hands—they looked calm, confident, and kind—a stark contrast to his face that was stern and unapproachable. I couldn't reconcile the two—the hands of a gentle person with the face of someone judgmental. To have such hands, I thought, he must have a warm, empathic heart. But he didn't share that with me, and thus I came to appreciate the directness of hands, how they reveal qualities not always visible in the face.

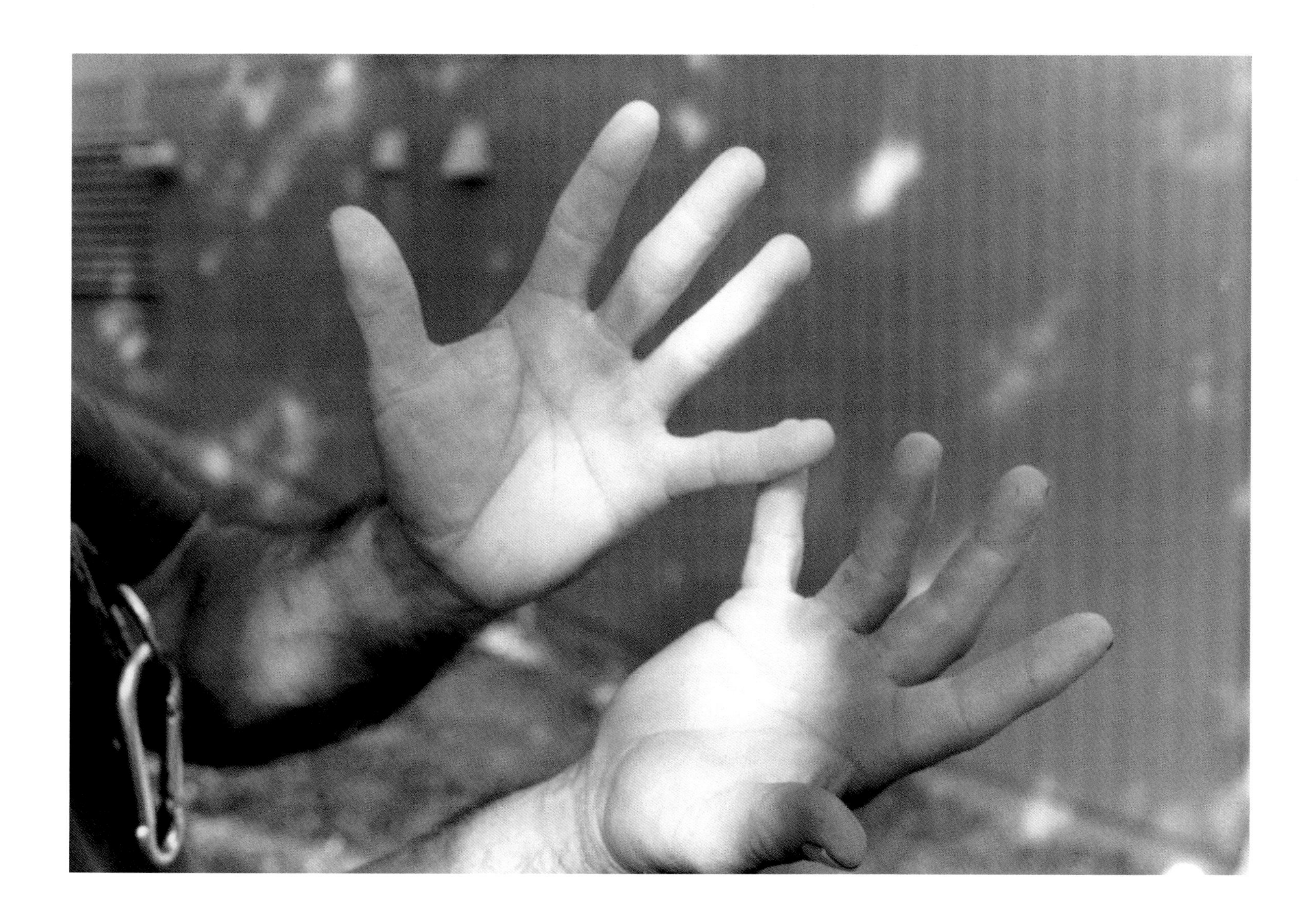

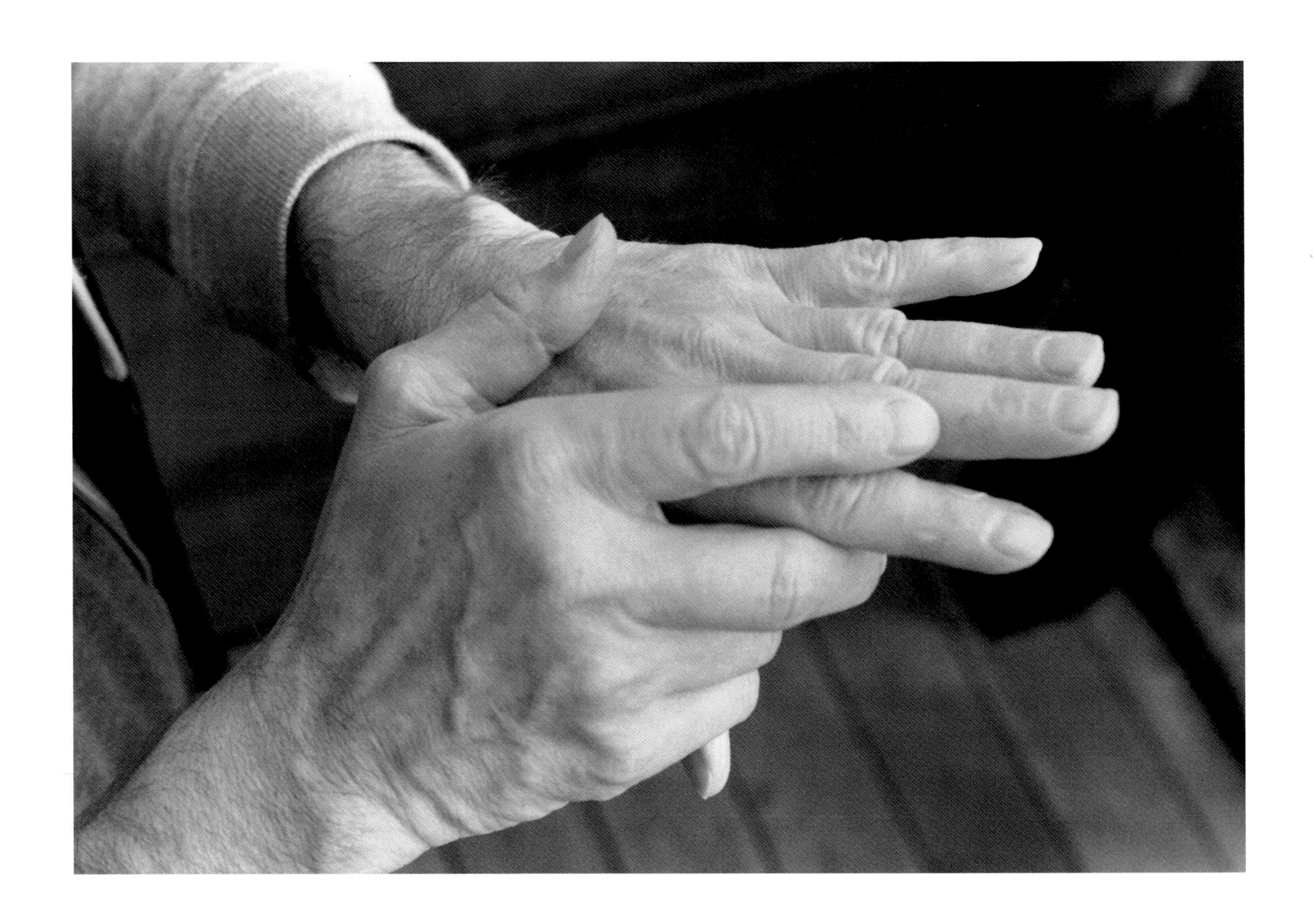

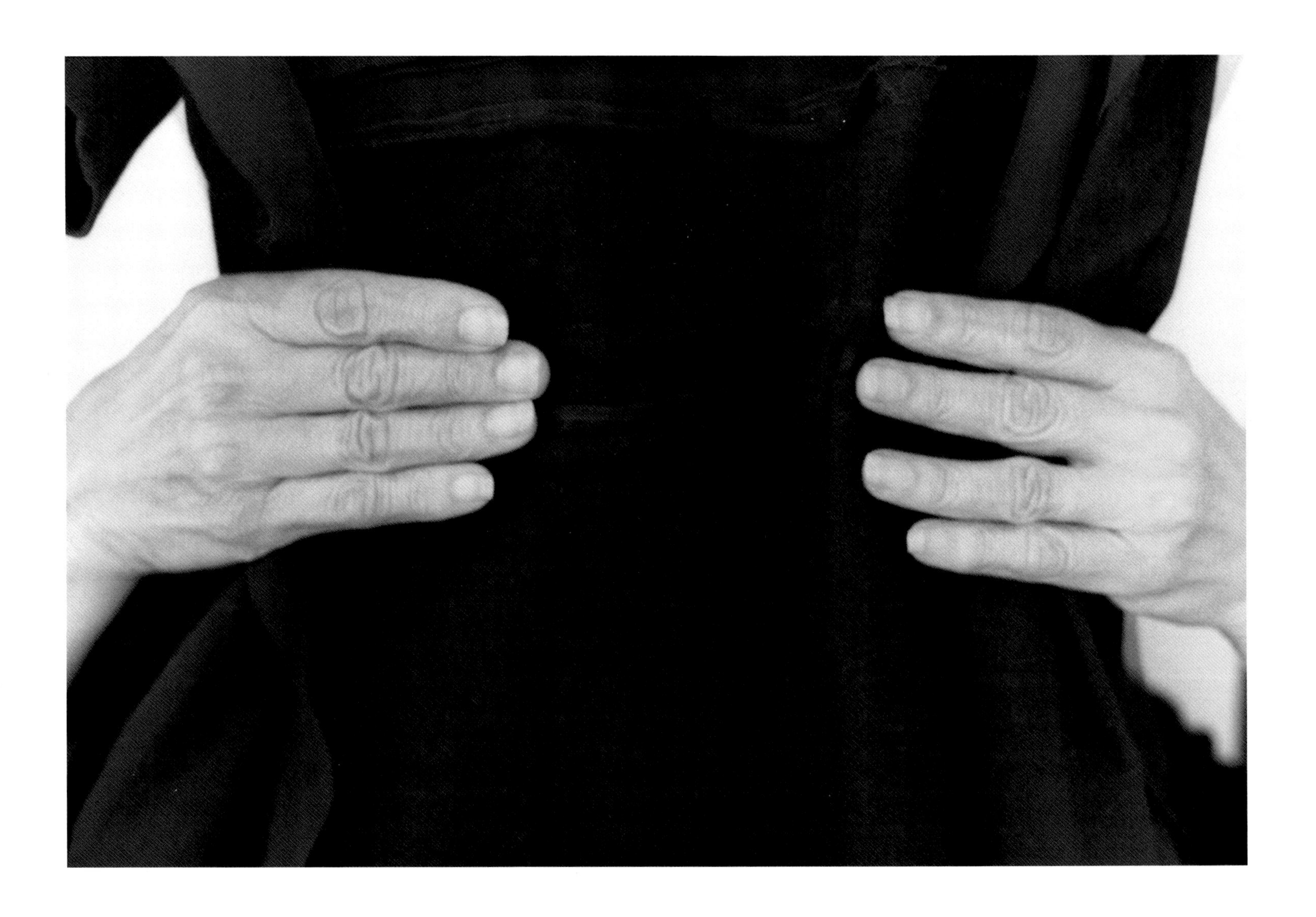

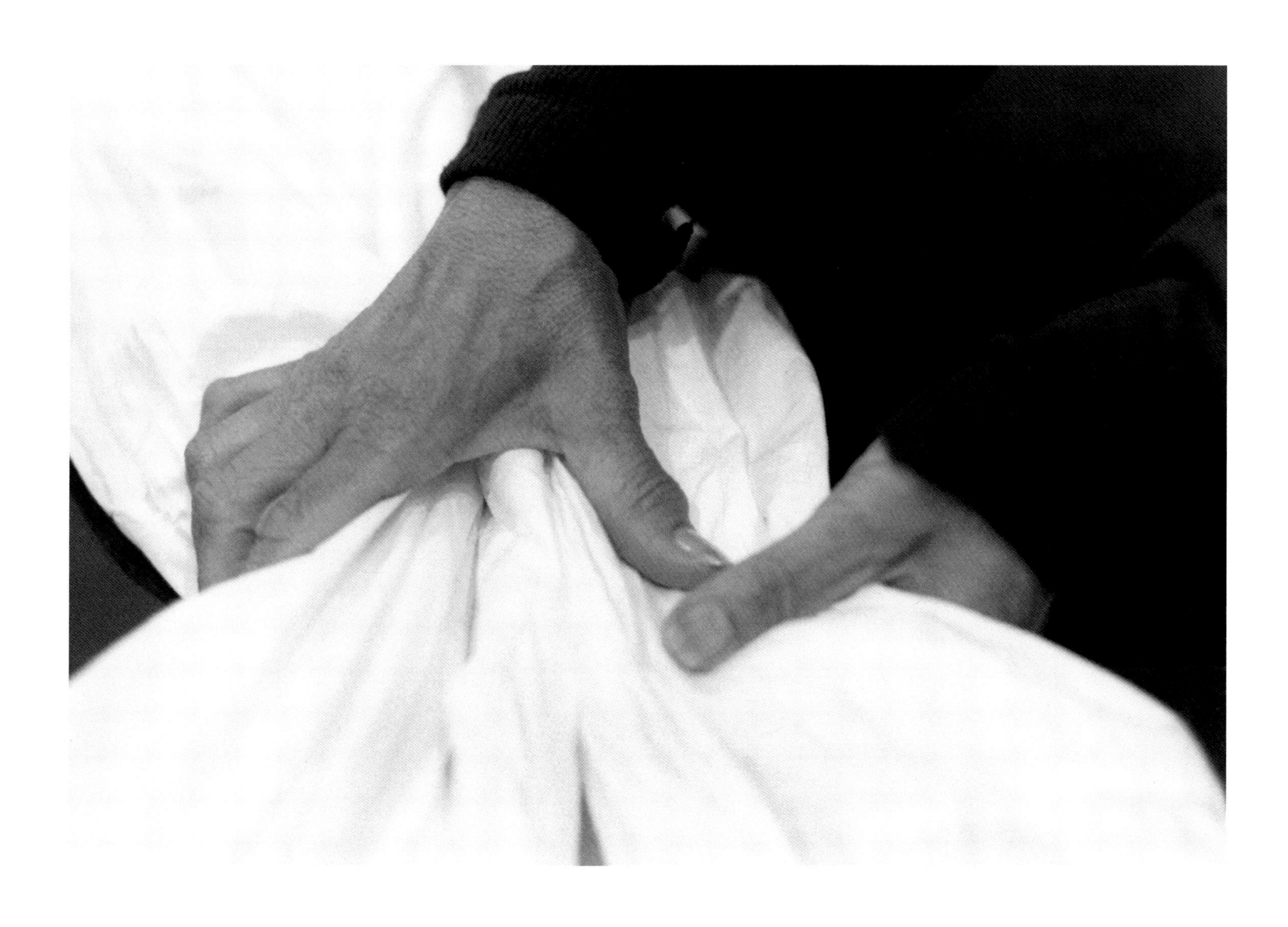

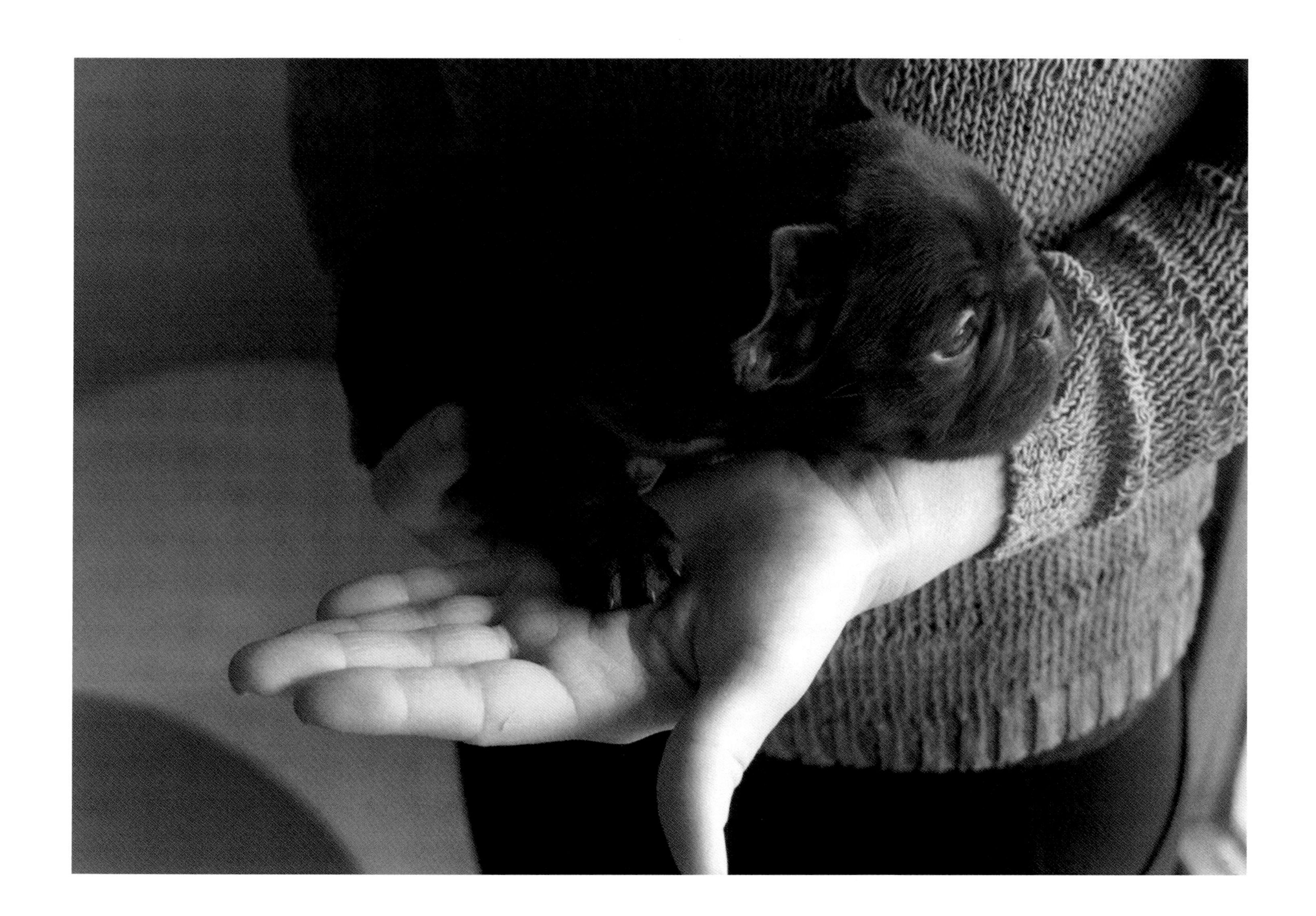

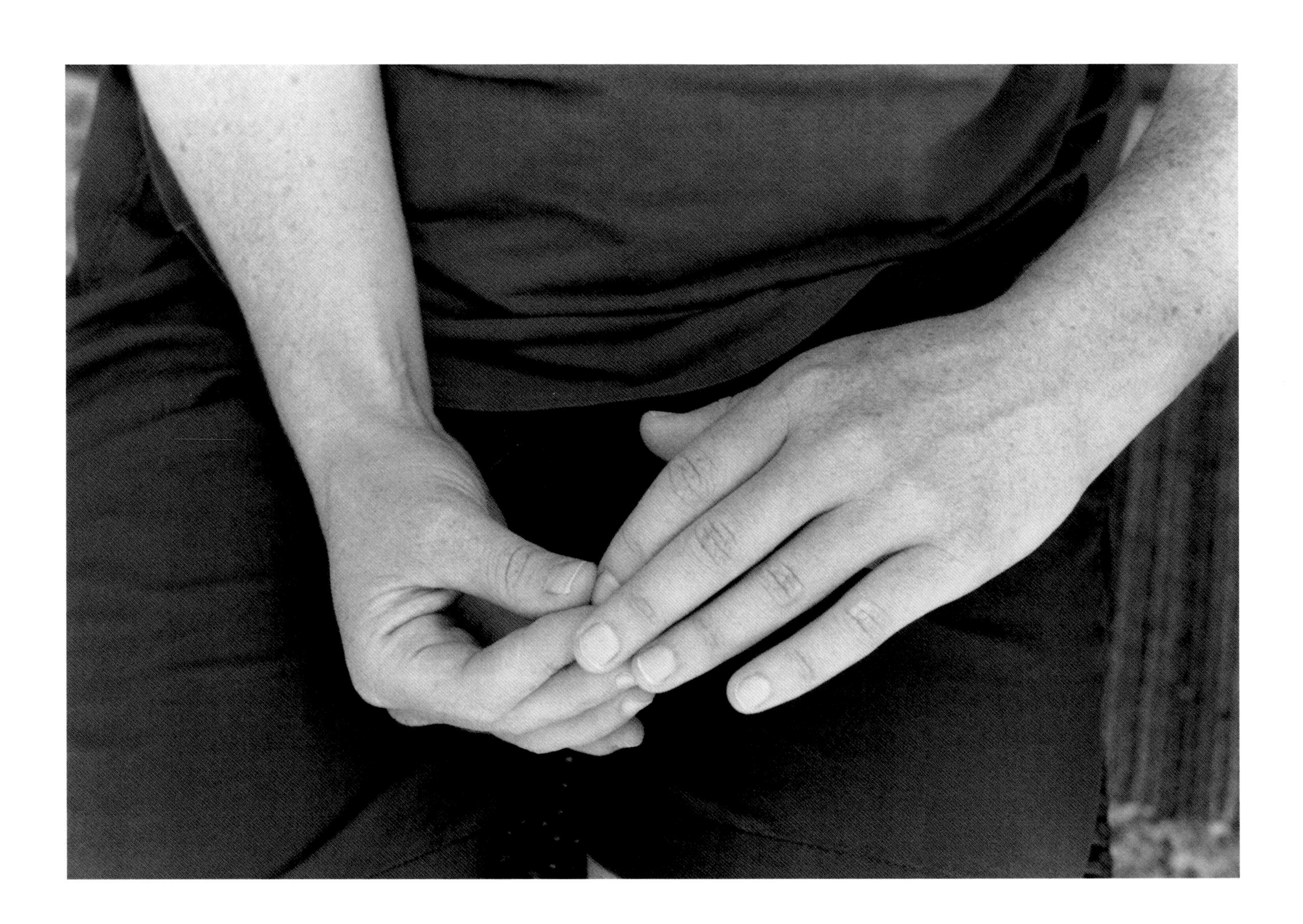

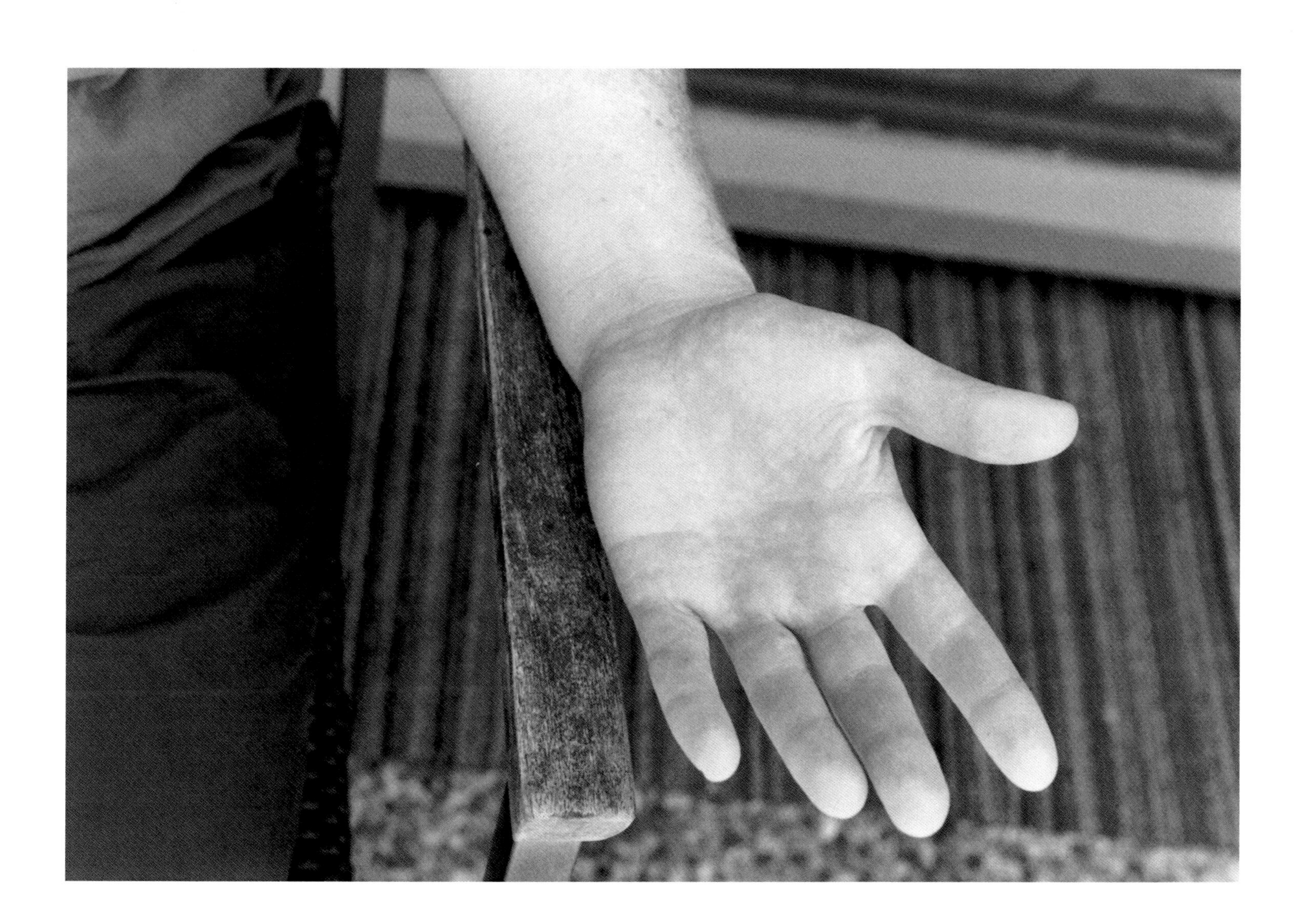

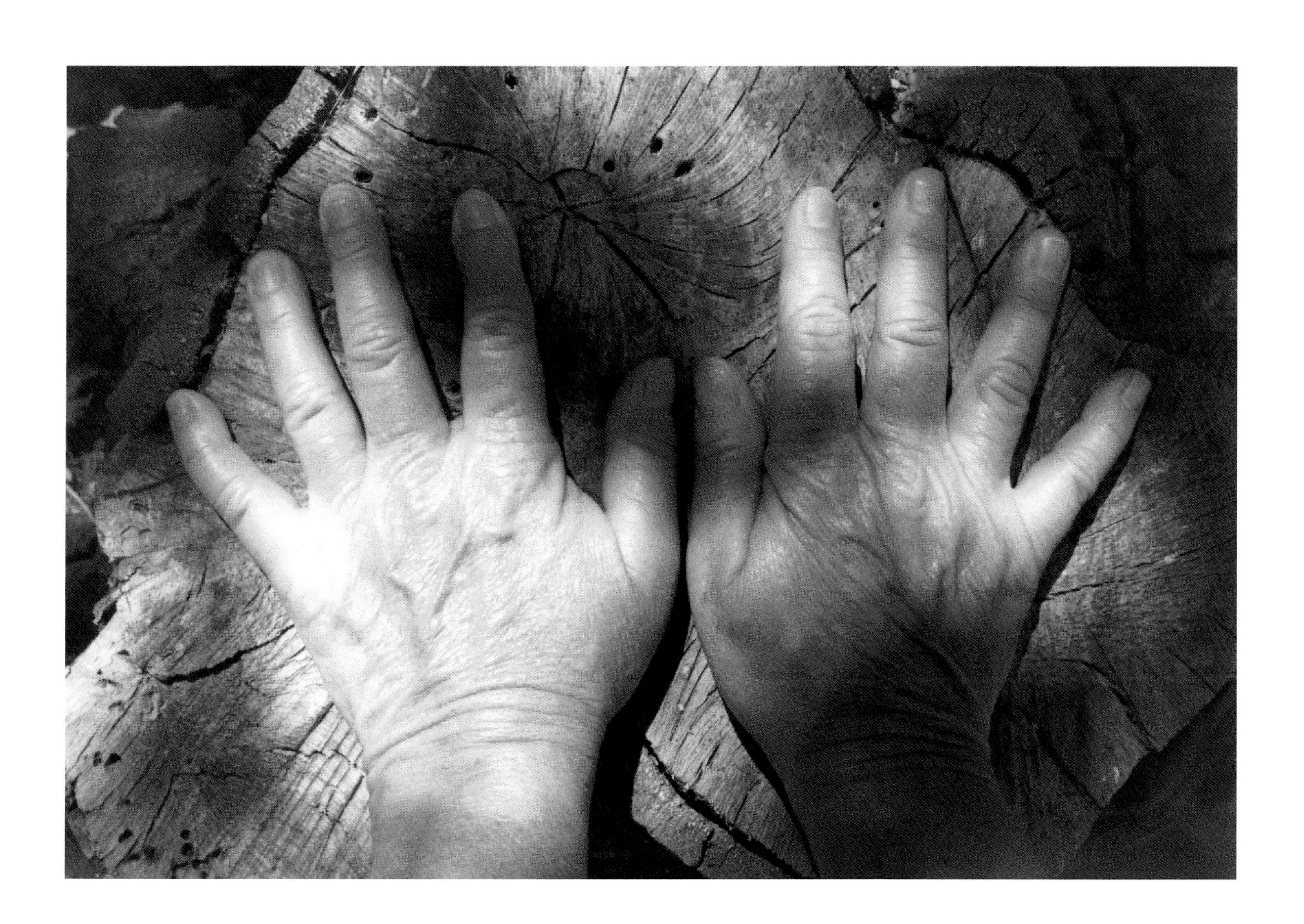

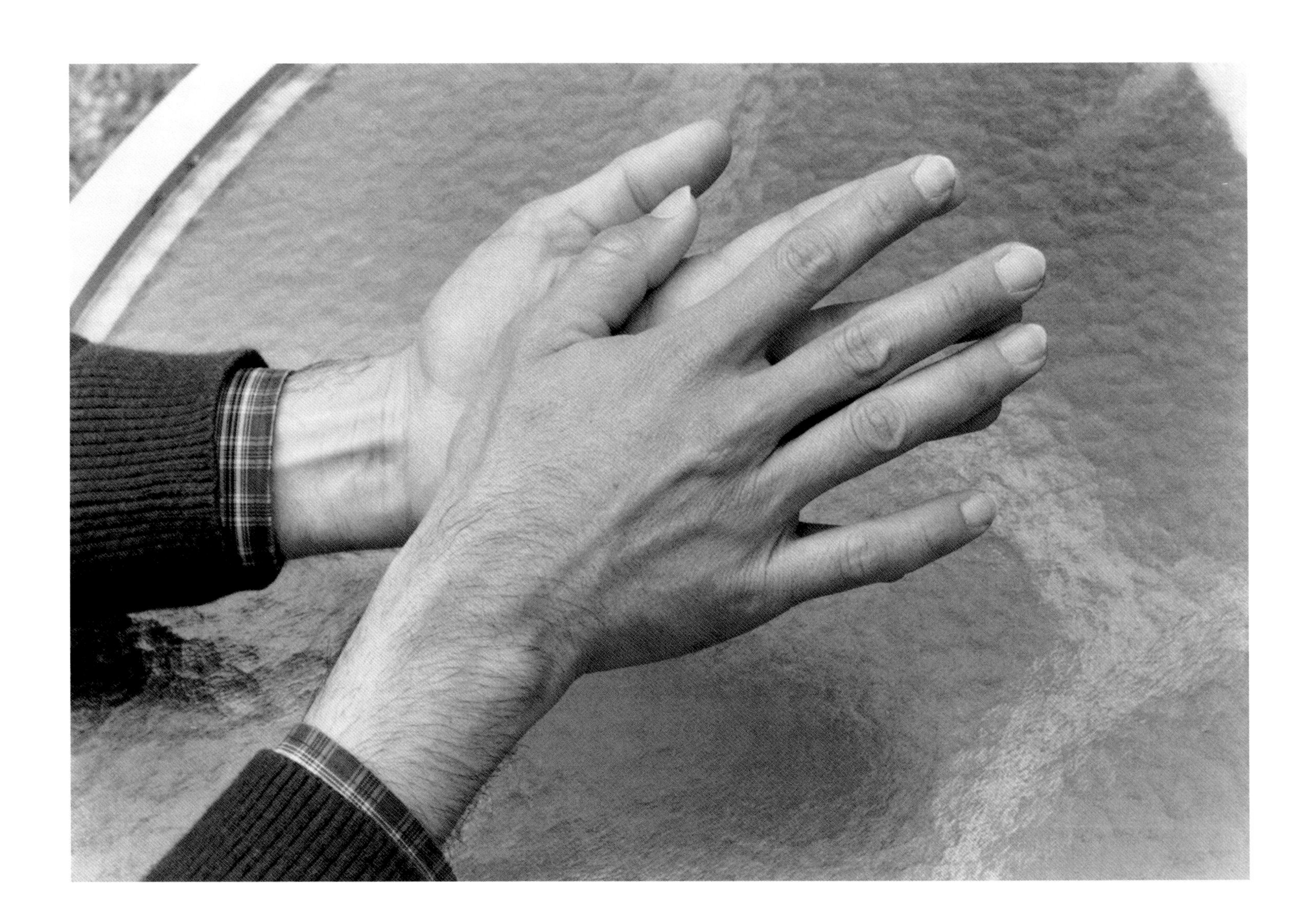

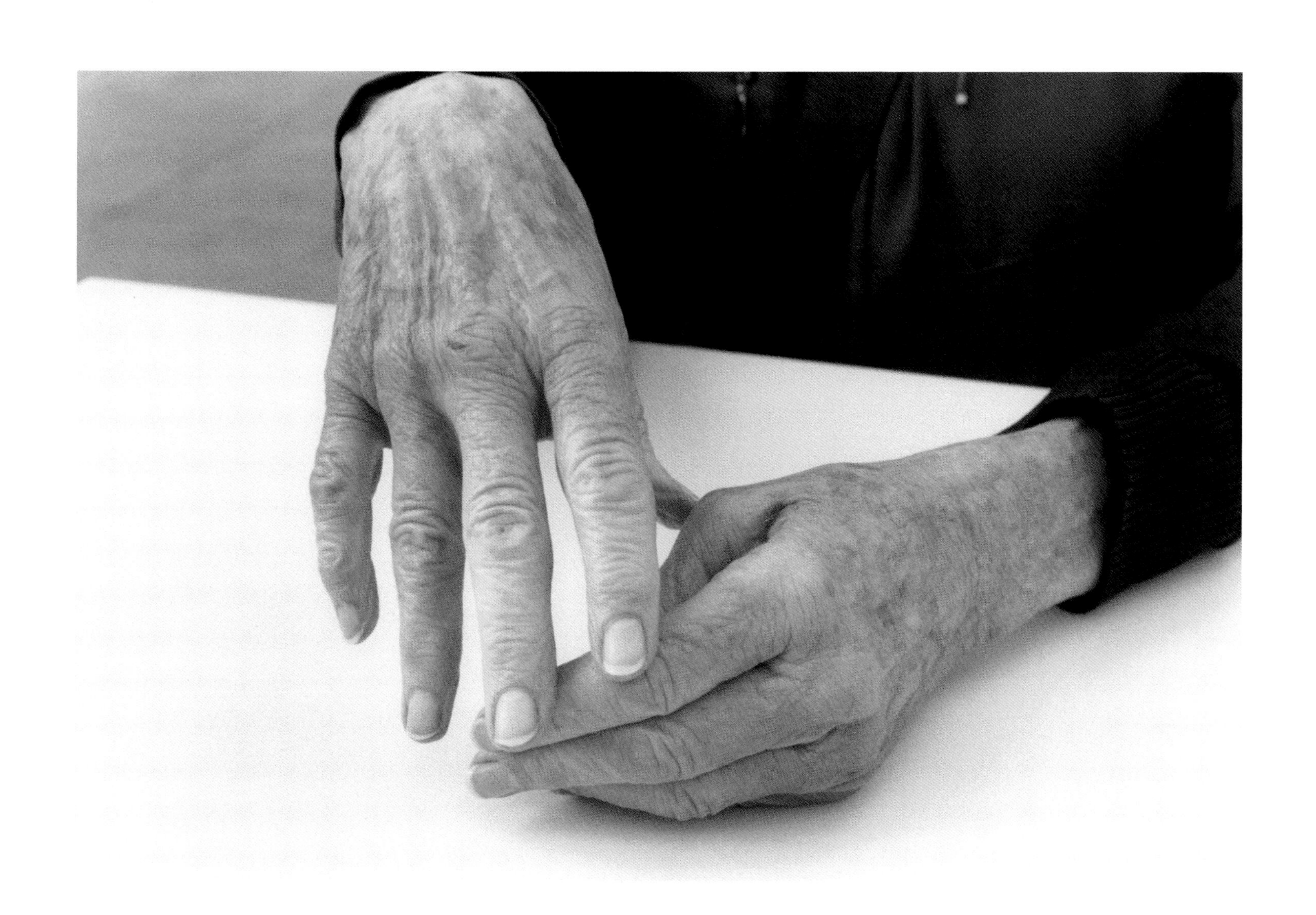

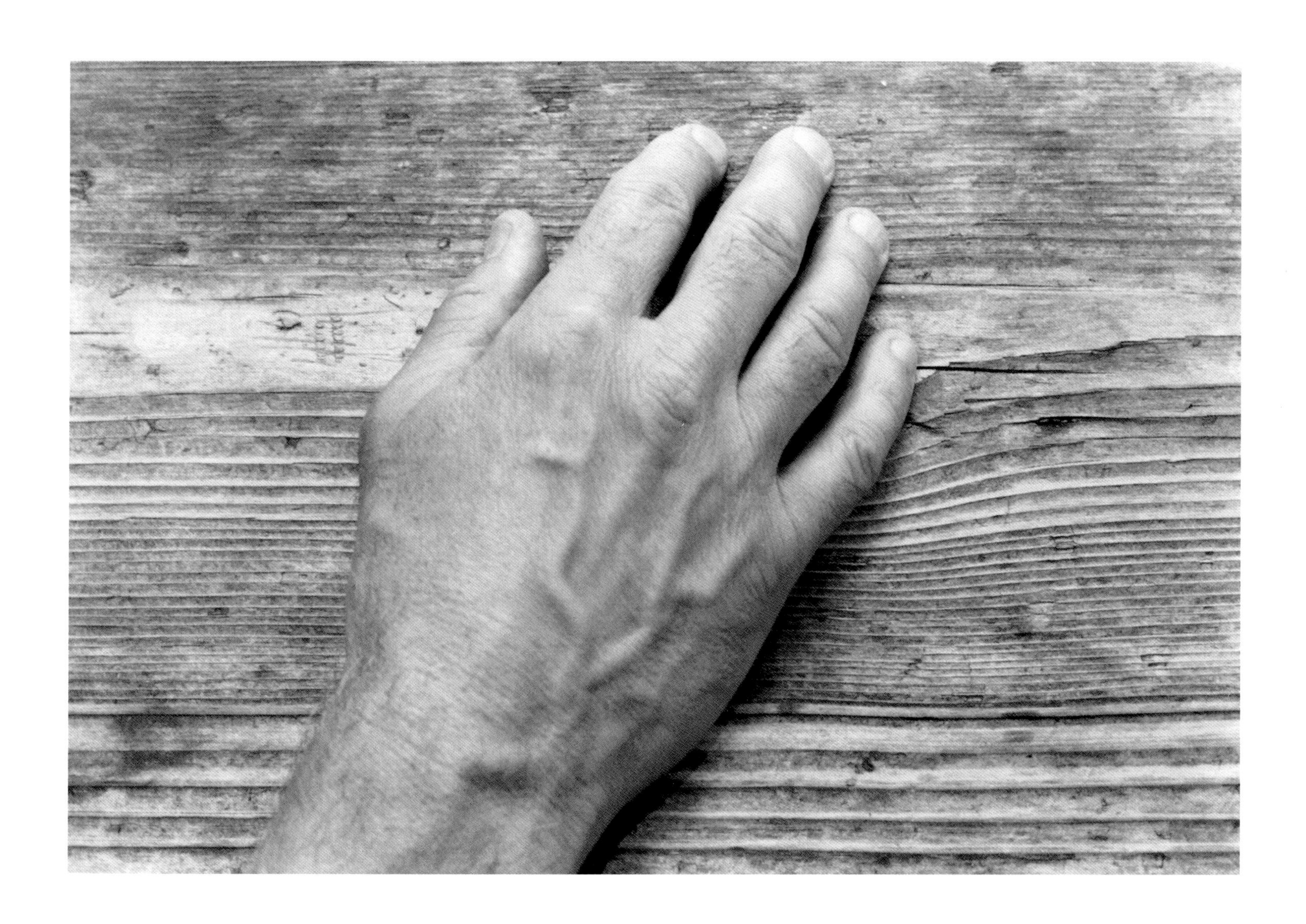

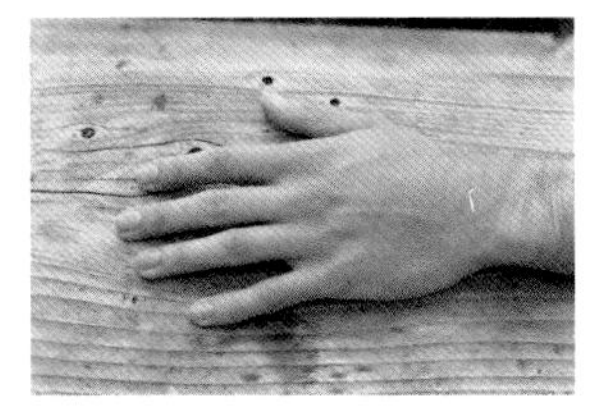

Myles, Lake Tahoe, 2020

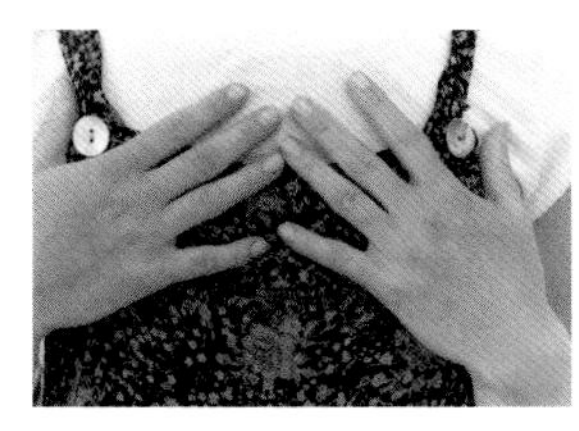

Miranda, Lake Tahoe, 2020

Luis (1), Portola Valley, 2020

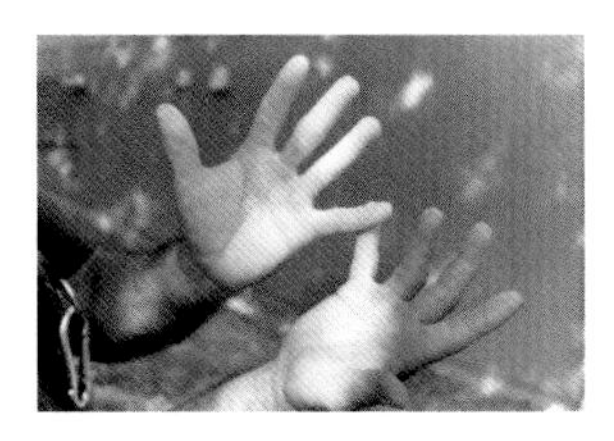

Luis (2), Portola Valley, 2020

Laurie, Portola Valley, 2020

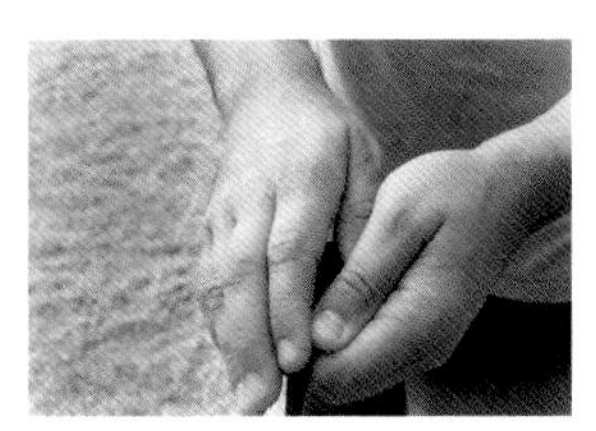

Ruben, Los Gatos, 2020

Roberta, Portola Valley, 2020

Chris (1), Portola Valley, 2020

Chris (2), Portola Valley, 2020

Alena, Menlo Park, 2020

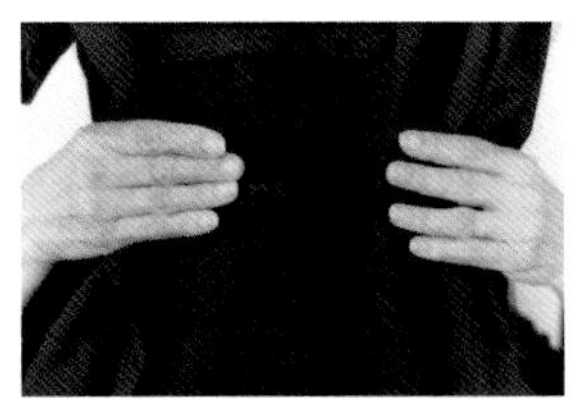

Mehri (1), Palo Alto, 2021

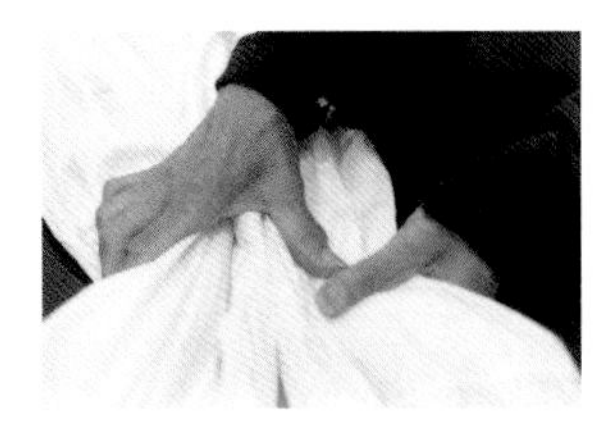

Mehri (2), Palo Alto, 2021

Stacy, Los Gatos, 2020

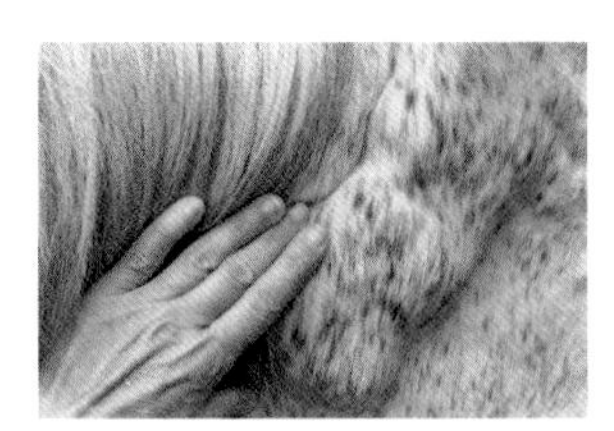

Sara, Buellton, 2020

Emily (1), Portola Valley, 2020

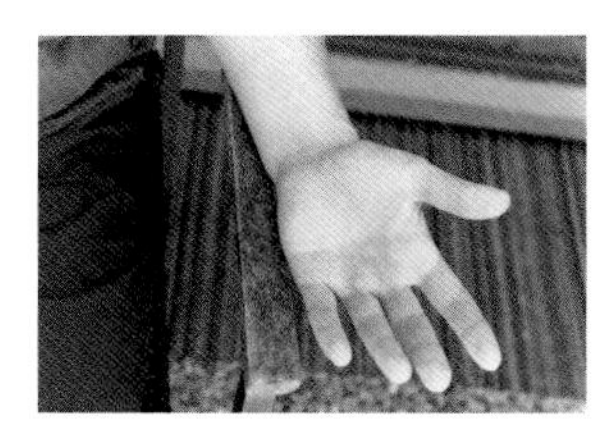

Emily (2), Portola Valley, 2020

Aidan, Portola Valley, 2021

Françoise (1), Woodside, 2020

Françoise (2), Woodside, 2020

Dale (1), Stanford, 2020

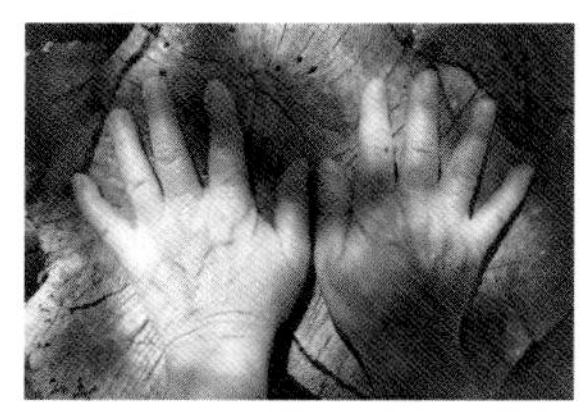

Dale (2), Stanford, 2020

Myles and Miranda, San Francisco, 2020

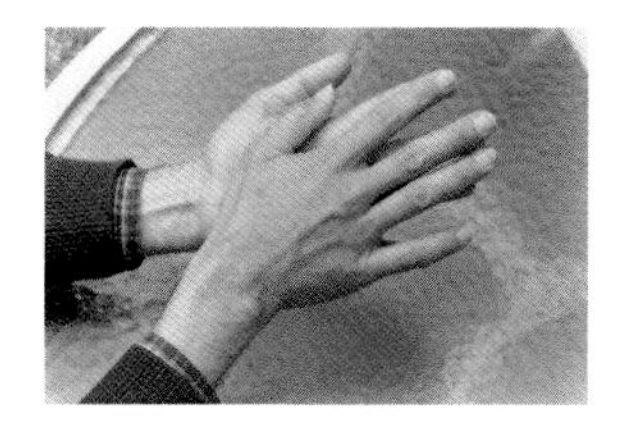

Rodrigo, Portola Valley, 2021

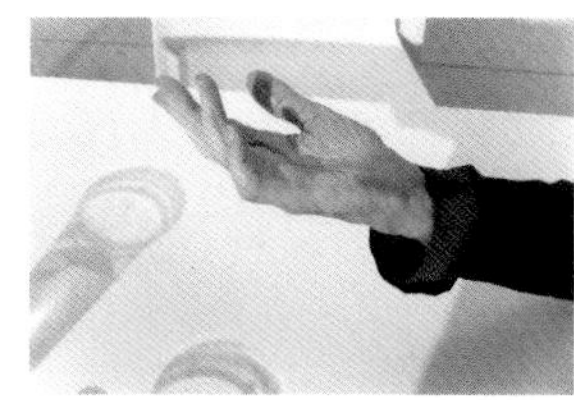

Paddy (1), San Francisco, 2020

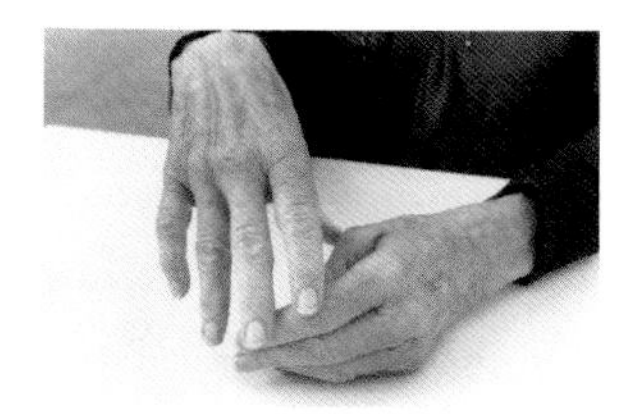

Paddy (2), San Francisco, 2020

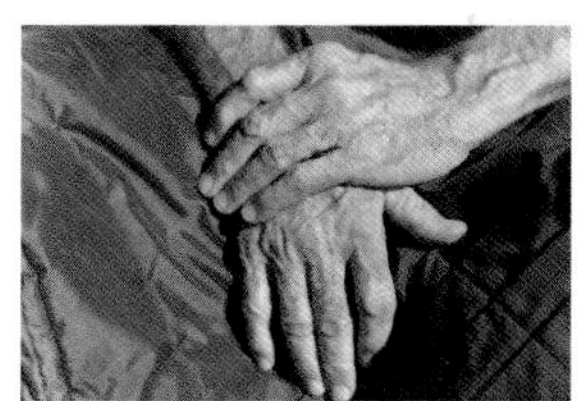

Philip (1), Portola Valley, 2020

Philip (2), Portola Valley, 2020

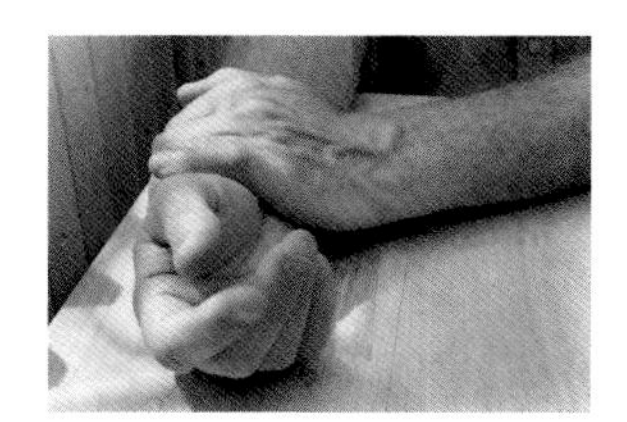

Scott, Brooklyn, 2021

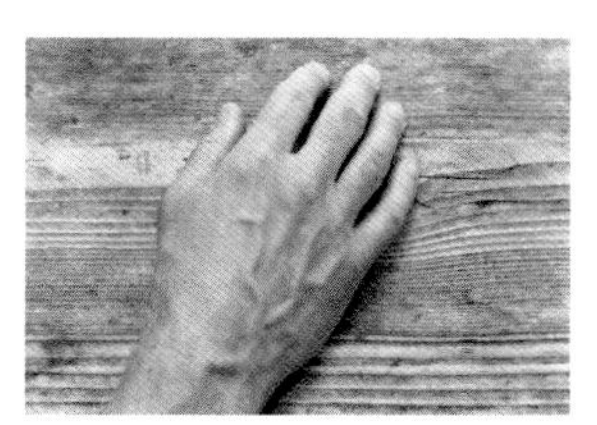

Scott, Lake Tahoe, 2020

WITHOUT MASKS

saraleith-tanous.com

First Edition 2021

Printed in the United States by Meridian Printing, East Greenwich, RI

BOOK DESIGN BY FRANCESCA RICHER